The Lord's Prayer

Our Father, who art in heaven,
hallowed be thy name.
Thy kingdom come,
thy will be done
on earth as it is in heaven.
Give us this day our daily bread
and forgive us our trespasses,
as we forgive those that trespass
against us.
And lead us not into temptation
but deliver us from evil,
for thine is the kingdom, the power
and the glory, for ever and ever.

Amen

This beautifully illustrated edition of The Lord's Prayer presents a sensitive combination of words and pictures to help children to a greater appreciation and understanding of this well loved prayer.

Another version of The Lord's Prayer used by many churches today is given at the back of the book.

First edition

LADYBIRD BOOKS, INC.
Lewiston, Maine 04240 U.S.A.
© LADYBIRD BOOKS LTD MCMLXXXVII
Loughborough, Leicestershire, England

Printed in England

The Lord's Prayer
for children

Illustrated by DEBBIE BOON-JENKINS

Ladybird Books

Our Father,
who art
in heaven,

*hallowed be
thy name.*

on earth
as it is
in heaven.

and forgive us our trespasses,

for thine is the kingdom,

*the power
and
the glory,*

*for ever
and ever.
Amen*

Some people say this version:

The Lord's Prayer

Our Father in heaven,
hallowed be Your name,
Your kingdom come,
Your will be done,
on earth as in heaven.
Give us today our daily bread.
Forgive us our sins
as we forgive those
who sin against us.
Do not bring us to the time of trial
but deliver us from evil.
for the kingdom, the power
and the glory are Yours
now and for ever.

Amen